Ye Olde RANSOM NOTE Sticker Book

For THINE ANONYMOUS Messages

E

K

L

R

Z

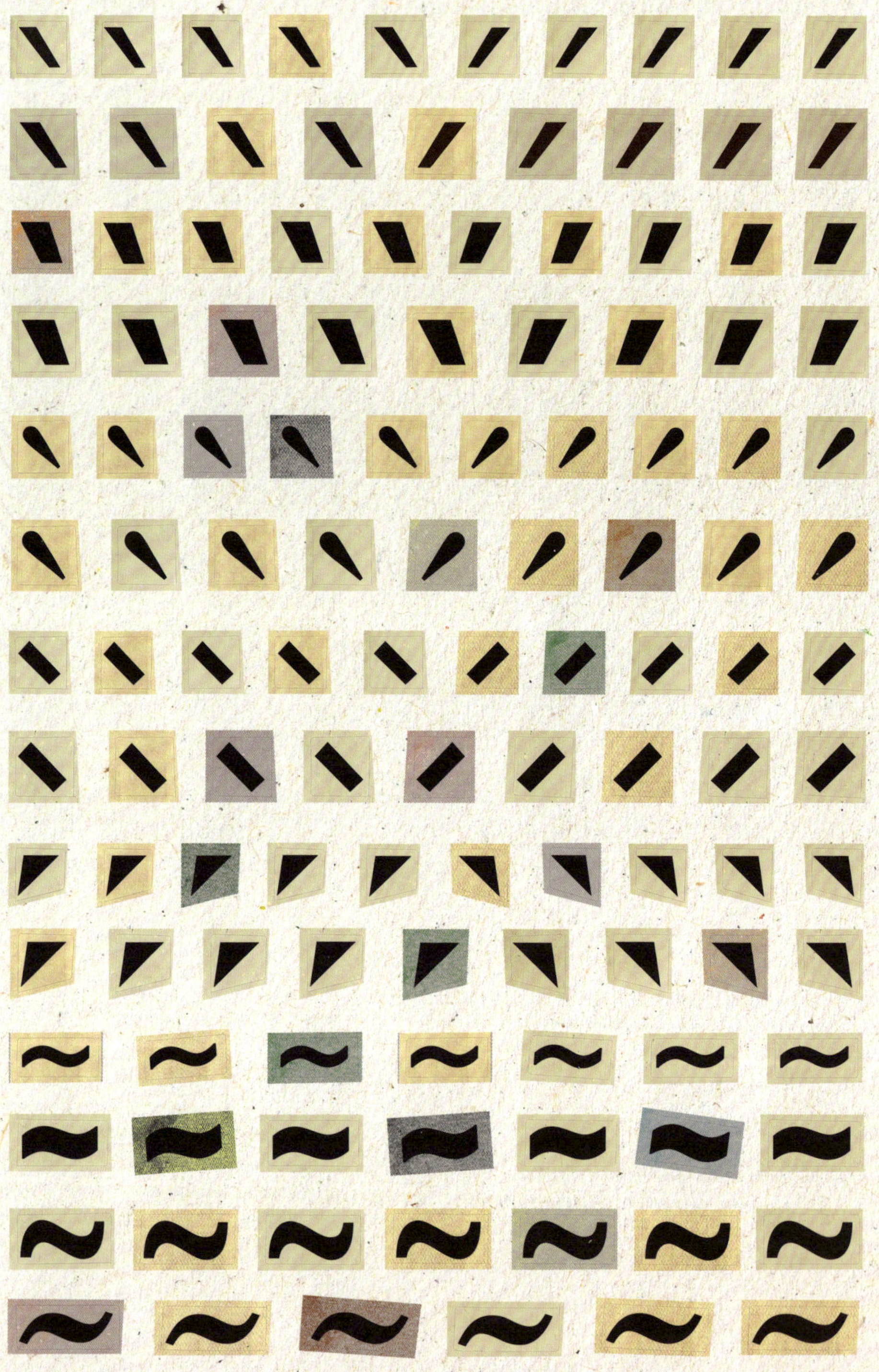

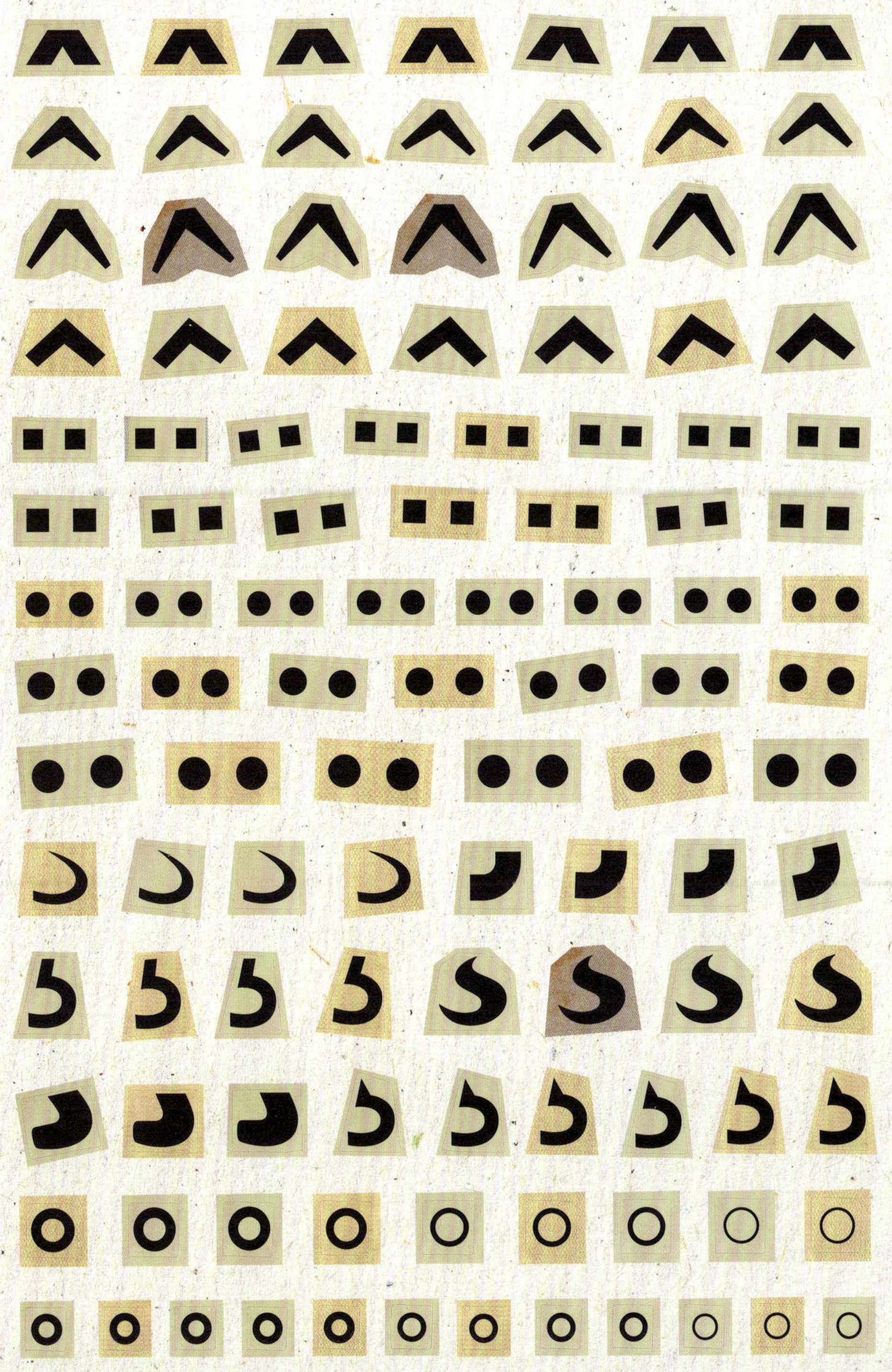

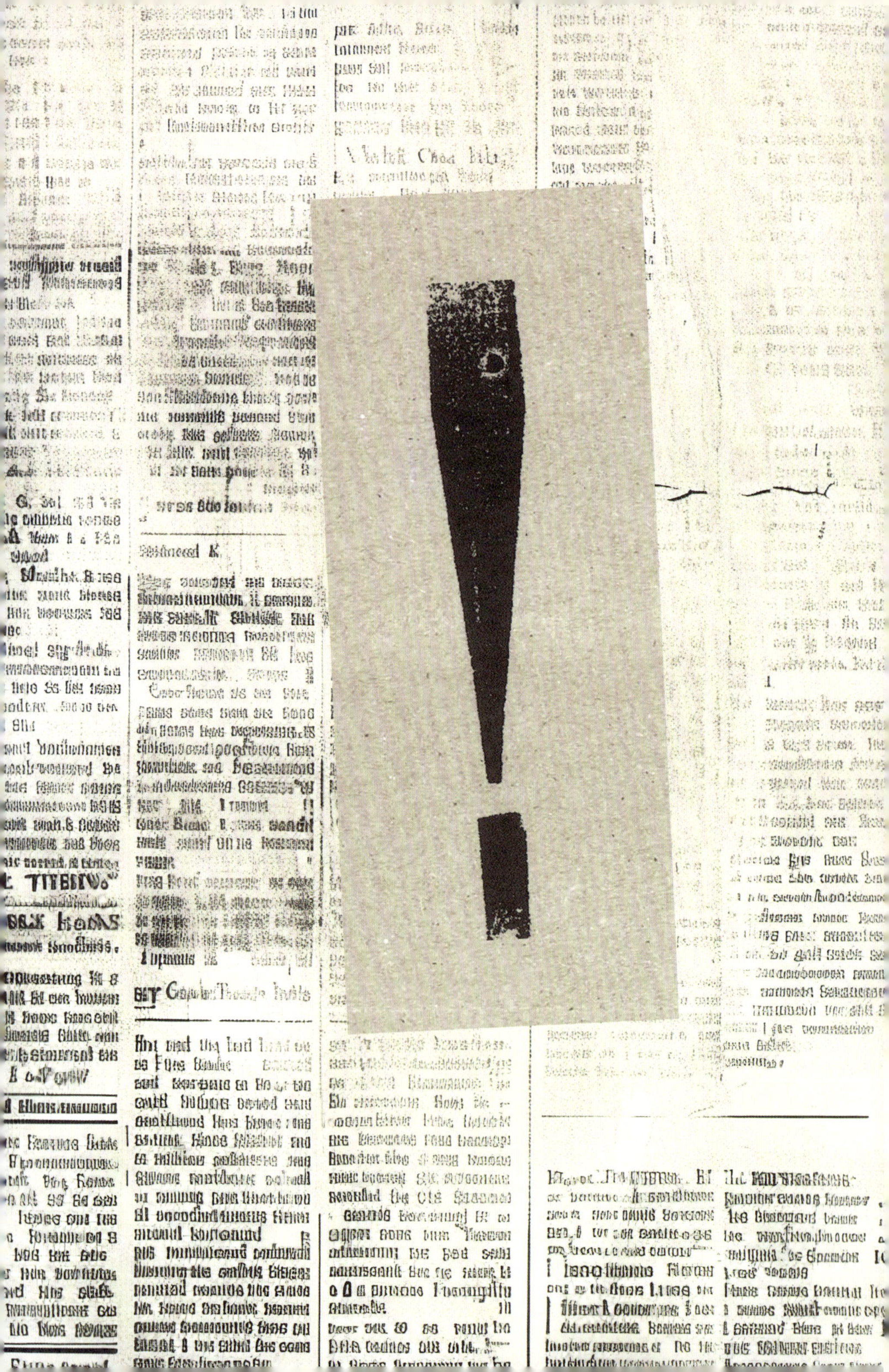

34

89

4 4 4 5 5
5 5 5 6 6
6 6 6 7 7
7 7 7 7 8
8 8 8 8 9
9 9 9 9

ihc
ihc

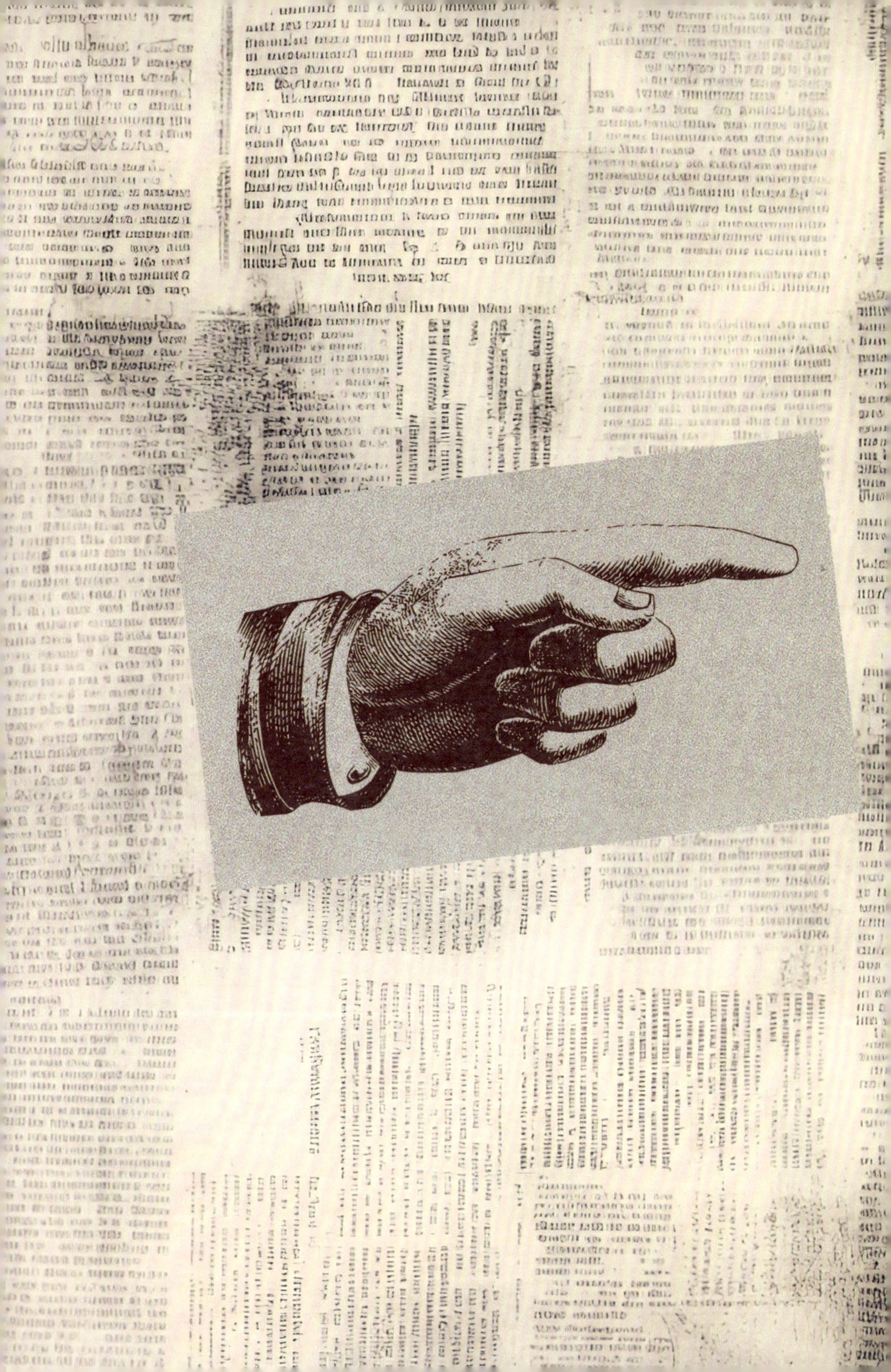

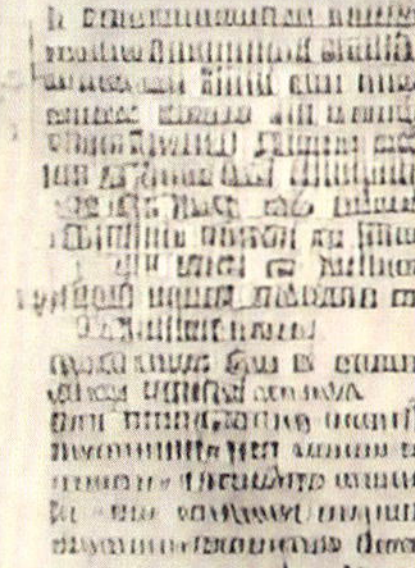

THE
The
The
THE
THE
The
the
The
of
of
of
AND
and
AND
and
AND
AND
and
and
AND

THE

END

First published in the United Kingdom in 2025 by Skittledog, an imprint of Thames & Hudson Ltd, 6–24 Britannia Street, London WC1X 9JD

Cover Design: Alison Guile
Designer: Luke Herriott
Production: Felicity Awdry

EU Authorized Representative: Interart S.A.R.L.
19 rue Charles Auray, 93500 Pantin, Paris, France
productsafety@thameshudson.co.uk
www.interart.fr

A CIP catalogue record for this book is available from the British Library

ISBN 978-1-83776-088-6
02

Printed and bound in China by Win Choi Printing

MIX
Paper from responsible sources
FSC® C156231

Be the first to know about our new releases, exclusive content and author events by visiting:

thamesandhudson.com
thamesandhudsonusa.com
thamesandhudson.com.au